Parent's Introduction

Whether your child is a beginning reader, a reluctant reader, or an eager reader, this book offers a fun and easy way to encourage and help your child in reading.

Developed with reading education specialists, **We Both Read** books invite you and your child to take turns reading aloud. You read the left-hand pages of the book, and your child reads the right-hand pages—which have been written at one of six early reading levels. The result is a wonderful new reading experience and faster reading development!

You may find it helpful to read the entire book aloud yourself the first time, then invite your child to participate the second time. As you read, try to make the story come alive by reading with expression. This will help to model good fluency. It will also be helpful to stop at various points to discuss what you are reading. This will help increase your child's understanding of what is being read.

In some books, a few challenging words are introduced in the parent's text with **bold** lettering. Pointing out and discussing these words can help to build your child's reading vocabulary. If your child is a beginning reader, it may be helpful to run a finger under the text as each of you reads. To help show whose turn it is, a round dot ● comes before text for you to read, and a star shape ★ comes before text for your child to read.

If your child struggles with a word, you can encourage "sounding it out," but keep in mind that not all words can be sounded out. Your child might pick up clues about a word from the picture, other words in the sentence, or any rhyming patterns. If your child struggles with a word for more than five seconds, it is usually best to simply say the word.

Most of all, remember to praise your child's efforts and keep the reading fun. After you have finished the book, ask a few questions and discuss what you have read together. Rereading this book multiple times may also be helpful for your child.

Try to keep the tips above in mind as you read together, but don't worry about doing everything right. Simply sharing the enjoyment of reading together will increase your child's reading skills and help to start your child off on a lifetime of reading enjoyment!

About Pets
A We Both Read Book
Level 1

Second Edition

For Maggie, Toto, Squeaky, and Bree—
my best friends.

Use of photographs provided by Getty Images, iStock, and Dreamstime.
Text Copyright © 2017, 2002 by Sindy McKay

We Both Read® is a trademark of Treasure Bay, Inc.

Published by
Treasure Bay, Inc.
P. O. Box 119
Novato, CA 94948 USA

Printed in China

Library of Congress Control Number: 2002103855

ISBN: 978-1-891327-42-1

Visit us online at:
WeBothRead.com

PR-6-21

About Pets

By Sindy McKay

TREASURE **BAY**

Dogs, cats, fish, birds, lizards, rats—pets are everywhere! They come in all different shapes, sizes, and colors.

★ Pets can be big.
Pets can be small.

Pets may have lots of soft, fluffy fur, or they may have rough, dry **scales**. Some pets have fins and some have wings.

★ This pet has **scales**.

● Different pets have different **needs**. Birds **need** a cage as a **place** to sleep, but most cats sleep anywhere they want to. A dog must be fed every day, but some snakes eat only once a week.

★ A dog **needs** a **place** to run. Most dogs like to run fast.

● Cats are one of the most popular pets in the world. They can be very loving and **purr** contentedly while curled up in your lap. However, they can also be very independent. Cats don't seem to mind being left alone while their owner is away at school or work.

★ Cats have soft fur. They may **purr** if you pet them.

● Dogs are also extremely popular pets. That could be because there are so many different kinds of dogs to choose from. Or it might just be because a **puppy** is too doggone cute to resist!

★ A **puppy** is a lot of fun to play with!

● Dogs and cats are
the two most common
household pets, but
there are many other
animals that make
great pets as well.
Some other favorite
four-legged friends
are rats, hamsters,
rabbits, guinea pigs,
and lizards.

★ This boy has a **rabbit** for a pet.

● Not all pets have four legs. Many people choose birds as pets, while others might choose fish or snakes.

★ Fish make good pets.
Cats like them, too!

● Pet owners try to spend as much time as possible with their pets, and **many talk** to them the same way they talk to a good friend.

★ **Many** pet birds can sing.
Some pet birds can even **talk**.

- The variety of pets available is vast and wonderful. But no matter which animal you choose as a pet, it must be well cared for and **loved.**

★ This dog **loves** to ride in the car.

- Owning a pet is a big responsibility. A pet cannot take care of itself. A pet's owner is responsible for providing good food for the pet along with plenty of fresh **water** to **drink**.

★ This is NOT a good
way to get a **drink**
of **water**!

Some pets may like to eat the same **food** we eat, but feeding "people **food**" to pets is not a good idea. They need to eat special **food** that has been made just for them.

★ Some dogs beg for **food**.
Some kids beg for food, too!

- Another important aspect of caring for a pet is making sure it gets enough exercise. Goldfish can take care of getting their own exercise, but providing toys for cats to **chase** and play with can help them get exercise.

★ Dogs love to play with
you. They love to jump
and **chase** balls.

Regular visits to the veterinarian will help assure that your pet stays healthy. A veterinarian can advise you on the right diet and exercise to keep your pet **happy** and give any necessary shots or medicine to prevent disease.

★ A well pet is a **happy** pet.

Most pets require some kind of grooming. Some must get regular haircuts and **baths.** Some may need to have their nails clipped and their teeth brushed.

★ Big dogs need big tubs for their **baths**.

Having a place to call home is important for every kind of pet. Birds need a large, clean cage. Fish live in an aquarium. Reptiles and snakes need a special enclosure with a heater to keep their body temperature steady.

★ This dog needs a big bed!

● All pets need the time and attention of their owners. Your pet might also want lots of affection.

★ Some pets love to get hugs, but some pets do not like hugs.

● If you are thinking of getting a pet, consider what
  kind of animal is right for you. How much time will
  you have to spend with your pet? How much money
  are you willing to spend on its care and upkeep?

★ A dog or cat makes a
good pet. So does a frog.

● Few things are **cuter** than a puppy, but a puppy can be a real handful! You might want to choose an older animal that's already been trained. If you're not going to be home much, consider getting two pets so they can keep each other company.

★ One dog is cute.
Two dogs are **cuter**!

It doesn't take long for pets to become part of our lives, and soon we wonder how we ever got along without them.

They join us at work and at play. They cheer us up when we're sad and share our joy when we're feeling happy.

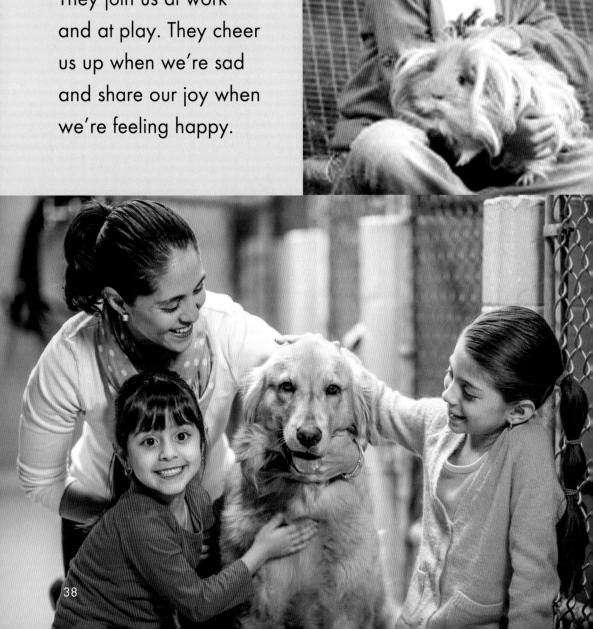

★ They play with us.
They even sing with us.

● If we are **very** good **friends** to our pets and give them what they need, they can give back to us lots of love and devotion and laughter.

★ A pet can be a **very** nice **friend**.

If you liked **About Pets** here are some other
We Both Read® books you are sure to enjoy!

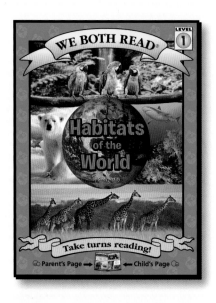

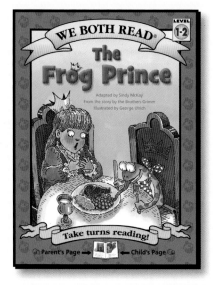

To see all the We Both Read books that are available,
just go online to **www.WeBothRead.com**.